Previous Page: Sunrise at Yaki Point in Grand Canyon National Park. David M. Morris.

Above: Louis Akins' 1906 oil painting, El Tovar, was purchased by the Santa Fe Railway for use in advertising.

Wotans Throne from Cape Royal, Grand Canyon. David M. Morris.

HOPI HOUSE

CELEBRATING 100 YEARS

◆ by Christine Barnes ◆

Acknowledgments

The author wishes to thank Carrie Compton, Barbara Fifer, and Linda McCray. Also, LaRee Bates, The Heard Museum; Bruce Brossman, Xanterra Parks and Resorts; James Garrison, Arizona State Historic Preservation Officer; Sally King, Santa Fe Archives; Kathryn Leonard, National Register Coordinator, Arizona State Parks; and James Woodward, Woodward Architectural Group. Particular thanks to Michael Quinn of the Grand Canyon Museum, whose assistance, interest, and enthusiasm are always appreciated.

First Edition 2005
Published by W.W.West, Inc.,
20875 Sholes Rd., Bend, Oregon

Copyright 2005 Text by Christine Barnes
Copyright 2005 Photos by photographers/insitution credited

Book Design: Linda McCray
Copy Editor: Barbara Fifer
Project Manager: Carrie Compton

Publisher's Cataloging-in-Publication Data is available upon request.

Printed in China by C&C Offset Printing Co. LTD.

Table of Contents

The Hopi House: Celebrating 100 Years

On January 1, 2005, the Hopi House celebrated its one-hundredth year. Built across the courtyard from the elegant El Tovar hotel, near the edge of the Grand Canyon's plummeting South Rim, the traditional Pueblo-style structure and the first-class hotel opened within days of each other.

Rail-blazing travelers had been taking the train to the South Rim since Locomotive 282 first brought them to the "Divine Abyss" on a spur of the Atchison, Topeka & Santa Fe Railway on September 17, 1901. The detour from Williams, Arizona, where they departed the Santa Fe's *California Limited* to Los Angeles and San Francisco and boarded the Grand Canyon Railway, served up an added opportunity for adventure. Awe-struck by the beauty of the canyon, they were often as stunned by the lack of creature comforts. Within four years, though, passengers no longer needed to settle for ramshackle hostels. Knowing that wealthy clientele demanded first-class accommodations, the railway hired Charles Whittlesey (1867-1941) to design a European villa with a distinctly western flair. The $250,000 El Tovar did not disappoint; the hotel offered tourists the ultimate in luxurious accommodations of the era within a rustic log, shingle, and stone structure.

Native employees stand on different levels of the Hopi House looking across the courtyard to El Tovar. Grand Canyon National Park Museum, No. 9648.

But across the dusty expanse of southwestern dirt, well-heeled tourists could dabble in perhaps their virgin exposure to the real American Southwest, at Hopi House. The juxtaposition of the rustic yet elegant hotel with what appeared to be authentic Indian dwellings gave travelers comfort coupled with intrigue.

The cool walls of Hopi House held a stunning array of Indian-made arts and crafts. Pottery and woodcarvings were artfully arranged on counters draped in hand-woven blankets and hand-loomed Navajo rugs. From the peeled log beams and the sapling, grass, and twig ceilings hung a plethora of woven baskets. Kachina dolls, ceremonial masks, and woodcarvings were casually arranged in dim rooms lightly washed in streaks of sunlight from tiny windows. Hopi murals decorated the stairway walls, and religious artifacts were part of a shrine room. Corner

Close up of the Hopi House reveals the beauty of its indigenous masonry. Xanterra, No. AH1969.

fireplaces, a piki oven, and rustic wooden tables and benches gave the feeling of a faraway home, not the Grand Canyon's first curio shop. And— tucked into alcoves and on the roof tops, creating their art, mingling, greeting or entertaining tourists, and even living in the upper floor—were Indians from neighboring pueblos.

The Santa Fe guaranteed exotic adventure to those ready to leave behind their familiar culture, pay $50 for a round-trip train ticket from Chicago to California, and travel by rail along the route of the historic Santa Fe trail. And with the able help of the Fred Harvey Company, they delivered. To travelers of the period, this was the real thing!

Hopi House, with its indigenous masonry, multiple roofs and mud-plastered interior walls, stands as the first example of the Grand Canyon work of designer and architect Mary Colter (1869-1958). The sales office, shop,

Pioneering tourists to the Grand Canyon could purchase Indian-made art, like this rug and basket from the early 1900s, at the Hopi House. Courtesy of the Heard Museum.

museum, living quarters, and artist's studio formed a daring departure from traditional regional architecture built by Anglos of the era. Colter interpreted the American Southwest not with the logs and stone of white pioneers as Whittlesey had done at El Tovar, but rather turned to the true homesteaders of the Grand Canyon: the Pueblo Indians. Hopi House was radically new to the traveling public, but the foundation of Mary Colter's Pueblo-inspired structure dates back ten thousand years to when Paleo-Indians traveled what is now the American Southwest in search of food. What eventually transpired was a settling of descendents of the prehistoric Pueblo Indians, who abandoned in part their nomadic life, and became the first successful dry-land farmers. The homes and villages of the region's Indians inspired Colter. The one-time Minnesota teacher had found her passion.

That passion was also embraced by

A young Mary Colter making a bowl.
Grand Canyon National Park Museum, No. 16952.

executives of the Santa Fe Railway along with those of the Fred Harvey Company. In 1876, when Edward Ripley, president of the Santa Fe, hired Fred Harvey to run the lunch counter in Topeka, Kansas, it was the beginning of a brilliant match. By 1899, Ripley formalized the agreement with the Fred Harvey Company as the railway's food service and hotel managers. The coupling of the Santa Fe and Fred Harvey Company not only changed customer service and accommodations for railway passengers, but also revolutionized the selling and advertising of the Southwest. And a major tool in that marketing portfolio was the use of the Native American people and their art. Themes of the Indians' rituals, ceremonies, and costumes, along with their harmony with the environment, dominated the Anglo interpretation of native life. A year after Fred Harvey officially signed on with the Santa Fe, Ripley promoted William Haskell Simpson to be the railway's general advertising agent. Simpson followed the lead of W.F. White and Charles Higgins, who first developed a Santa Fe advertising scheme, and he ran with it.

In 1892, the Santa Fe invited noted landscape artist Thomas Moran (1837-1926) to the Grand Canyon. Moran had first accompanied explorer John Wesley Powell on his survey of the Colorado River canyon, and found the spectacle "...the most awfully grand and impressive scene that I have ever yet seen."

Thomas Moran sketching the canyon with his daughters nearby, circa 1905. Grand Canyon National Park Museum, No. 12005.

Moran's *The Grand Canyon of the Colorado* painting, bought outright by the Santa Fe, became the catalyst of the railway's advertising campaign. That painting, reproduced and distributed throughout the country, introduced thousands of Americans to the canyon's grandeur. (Moran's earlier work is credited with opening the eyes of Congress, enabling the establishment of Yellowstone, the country's first national park, in Wyoming.)

The Santa Fe Railway brought artists and writers to locales along its line. Oftentimes Simpson traded transportation, food and lodging for their work, and the railway began acquiring an impressive collection that they used for calendars, brochures, beautifully illustrated books, and promotional lithographs.

Paintings by Louis Akin (1868-1913), E. Irving Couse (1866-1936), Bertha Menzler Dressler (1871-1947), Bert Geer Phillips (1868-1956), and Frank

Paul Sauerwein (1871-1910) were among art purchased by the Santa Fe. Many of these people joined artists' colonies, turning the Southwest into a Mecca for the arts. In search of reflecting their own country instead of the European ideal, these artists were inspired by more than the profoundly moving landscapes, and found some of their favorite subjects to be the first Americans. Men such as Akin and Sauerwein were particularly comfortable with the Hopi Indians, and became fast friends with their subjects. Louis Akin's 1906 oil painting, *El Tovar*—of

Facing Page: The awe of the canyon and curiosity about Indian culture were common advertising themes, facing page. Grand Canyon National Park Museum, No. 22567.

Selling wares to tourists. Courtesy Palace of the Governors, Museum of New Mexico, No. 46936.

the hotel, Hopi House and Indians, set along the pastel hues of the canyon—was a popular marketing piece.

While the Santa Fe was becoming a patron of Anglo-American artists, the Fred Harvey Company was most inter- ested in native arts, crafts, and jewelry. Collectors and tourists traditionally had bought Indian arts and crafts from creators selling their goods along the rail lines. The man behind the Fred Harvey Company's Indian trade was Herman Schweizer, who began a network between Indian artists and Fred Harvey outlets. By 1901, the Fred Harvey Indian Department, managed by Schweizer but the brainchild of Minnie Harvey Huckel, was established. Minnie's husband, John F. Huckel, was the Fred Harvey executive who headed the new department. That same year, Fred Harvey died, but his sons, Ford and Byron, and son-in-law, John, assumed his role overseeing hotels, restaurants, shops, and railway dining cars with a shared passion for the Southwest as a tourist destination.

The expanded theme of the southwestern stage was set and ready for an architecture style to match the region's growing lure.

TITAN of CHASMS

The Grand Canyon of Arizona

Below: Mary Colter (on right) reviewing construction plans for Bright Angel Lodge in 1935.
Grand Canyon National Park Museum, No. 16942.

Facing Page: Portrait of a young Mary Colter. Grand Canyon National Park Museum, No. 16950.

Mary Colter Arrives

This was the world that Mary Colter entered in 1902. A young midwesterner, Colter had been fascinated with Indian art even as a child. Remarkably, she held onto drawings created in 1877-1878 by Sioux prisoners from the Battle of the Little Bighorn, which she had received as a little girl. But it was at the California School of Design in San Francisco where she added architecture to her interests. According to Virginia Gratten, Colter's first biographer, the young woman worked as an apprentice at an architect's office while taking art and education classes. California's architectural community then was embracing Spanish Revival architecture, which Colter coupled with her love of Indian art to form a personal vision. But she had been sent to art school to earn a living, so she returned to St. Paul and a successful fifteen-year career teaching (predominantly freehand and mechanical drawing at Mechanic Arts High School) that helped support her widowed mother and sisters. Colter's life was full with outside art, lecturing on art and architecture, volunteer work, and continuously pursuing her passion for self-education.

Scholars are unsure of exactly how this school teacher met with the Fred Harvey Company, whether through art circles in St. Paul or on a trip to San Francisco, but the result is as solid as her marvelous work still standing at the Grand Canyon.

Mary Colter's first Fred Harvey commission was to decorate the company's Indian Building next to the Santa Fe's

The designs of the Southwest Indians were an inspiration throughout Colter's life. Xanterra, No. AH1964.

Alvarado Hotel—designed by Charles Whittlesey—and depot in Albuquerque, New Mexico. The Santa Fe was adapting the Spanish revival motif in its buildings as appropriate for stops along its transcontinental line to California. As the interior decorator for the rambling building, Colter created a series of intimate individual tableaus where tourists viewed the Harvey collection of archaeological finds and art pieces in a museum area, passed a Hopi religious altar, then wandered by the "living" museum—where Colter added Indians dressed in traditional Navajo clothing demonstrating their skills—and on to the curio shop to purchase carefully selected creations.

Her Albuquerque work completed, Colter returned to teaching in St. Paul, but her association with the Santa Fe Railway and Fred Harvey Company had just begun.

Mary Colter's interior decorations of the Indian Building in Albuquerque, New Mexico. Courtesy
Palace of the Governors, Museum of New Mexico, No. 1507.

Hopi House (1905)

The Santa Fe Railway and Fred Harvey Company executives had their eyes on developing the south rim of the Grand Canyon. In 1904, they commissioned Whittlesey to design El Tovar hotel, and contacted Colter to create an "Indian building" across the courtyard. The pair collaborated, both shunning the Spanish revival style and designing two remarkable buildings that reflected their individual talents and tastes and met the needs of their sponsors.

This time, Colter was not only designing the interior, but also creating the entire package. Her inspiration came one hundred miles east of the Grand Canyon, from the Oraibi Pueblo of the Hopi Indians. The Hopi, part of the modern Pueblo Indians, built terraced houses whose earthy design fascinated Colter. Founded about A.D. 1150, Oraibi Pueblo stands as the oldest continuously inhabited settlement in the United States.

"Colter did not copy history but fashioned her environments from their essence, relying on her well-rounded artistic talents, practical bent, and sense of humor to work historical reference into buildings constructed with modern methods and material," writes Arnold Berke in his book, *Mary Colter: Architect of the Southwest* (2002).

Colter's idea to fashion Hopi House after a Hopi dwelling was perfect for the Fred Harvey purpose of educating potential collectors, and selling arts and crafts for tourists' homes. The native work offered complementary additions to the Arts & Crafts–inspired homes and décor back in the East and Midwest, and the individual rooms and work settings within Hopi House set the stage for Colter's forte in interior design.

Although Colter technically worked for Fred Harvey, her structural designs and drawings were approved and sent

Oraibi Pueblo, 1897. Denver Public Library, Western History Collection, No. X30741.

to the Santa Fe Railway's Western Division offices in Los Angeles, where working plans were drawn and signed by railway architects. This process would continue throughout her career with the Santa Fe and Fred Harvey Company. And, while Colter conceived of the Hopi House design and was its

architect, John F. Huckel invited archaeologist and missionary H.R. Voth to participate in Hopi House to "ensure an accurate creation of Hopi architecture." Voth also worked with Herman Schweizer and the Fred Harvey Indian Department in amassing its collection of artifacts and arts. It was Voth who

The Hopi House with ladders depicting the traditional roof entrance was built with a front door to accommodate tourists. Grand Canyon National Park Museum, No. 11422.

designed the controversial altars within Hopi House.

Hopi Indians did much of the construction and masonry. Built of limestone, the three-story building with its multiple roofs, terraces, and stone steps was faced with sandstone blocks that supplied its distinctive reddish color. Colter did forgo the Hopi's traditional roof entrance to the dwelling, instead creating a front door for easy access to the treasures inside, and she added an interior stairway. The mud-finished inside walls, ceiling beams, and branch-covered ceilings characterized a Hopi home. Chimneys were made from ollas (pottery water jars), broken and stacked then mortared together. In addition to the display and sales "Indian" rooms, including a Totem Room with hand carved ceremonial masks and space for Northwest Coastal Indian art, was the Spanish-Mexican room where sombreros, spurs, a caballero's saddle, and firearms were displayed.

Images of southwestern destinations and art had been successfully promoted at world's fairs and expositions. At the 1904 Exposition in St. Louis, the Fred Harvey Navajo blanket and Pomo

A stone pillar at Mary Colter's Hermit's Rest appears to grow out of the canyon itself.
Xanterra, No. AH2295.

basket exhibits had each won prizes, and these, along with the company's archaeological collection, became the centerpiece for the museum exhibit on Hopi House's second floor. The third floor served as tiny apartments for Hopi artisans working there. Some of these artisans worked during the day in full view of tourists, creating the goods they desired, then joined other Hopi to spend evenings entertaining guests with native songs and dances.

The Hopi House and its collection and wares, demonstration areas, and Hopi residents and artisans were a huge success.

When Hopi House opened, Colter's work was completed at the Grand Canyon and, once again, she returned to St. Paul.

In 1910, when Colter was forty-three, the Fred Harvey Company offered her a permanent position as designer and architect, but her next project was not at the Grand Canyon. Instead, she spent the next few years working on the interiors of El Ortiz hotel in Lamy, New Mexico, and Harvey restaurants. She worked out of the Kansas City office, but her heart was still at the Grand Canyon.

A constant student, she traveled and studied, absorbed then created, everything from buildings to dishware. Her extraordinary knowledge of environmentally integrated, site-appropriate architecture was displayed in her designs for Hermit's Rest and Lookout Studio. Rather than embracing an Indian motif, she worked with the sheer cliffs and adrenalin-pumping panoramas of the canyon itself.

Hermit's Rest (1914)

In 1913, Colter submitted drawings for Hermit's Rest, situated on and seemingly growing out of the canyon's rim. Constructed of native stone, Hermit's Rest along the Santa Fe's trail into the canyon offered the Fred Harvey Company a chance to offer food and drink. Tucked into a man-made mound of stone, from its outside the structure looked like a haphazard pile of rocks. A broken mission bell and lantern clarified its use. Inside, a large porch, gigantic fireplace within a stone arch, rustic wooden beams and posts, heavy wrought iron, and log chairs gave the impression that, indeed, this was the home of a hermit. But huge glass windows looking out on the canyon gave a very different impression.

Above Left: The rock arch and mission bell still welcome travelers to Hermit's Rest.
Grand Canyon National Park Museum, No. 7512.
Above Right: The Great Fireplace at Hermit's Rest. Grand Canyon National Park Museum, No. 8497
Below Left: One of the historic Colter cabins at Phantom Ranch. Xanterra.
Below Right: Three visitors outside the original Phantom Ranch Lodge, 1925,
Grand Canyon National Park Museum, No. 04970.

Lookout Studio (1914)

Originally called The Lookout, Colter's observation post and curio shop respected both the environment and the clients who visited it. As noted in a 1917 Working Plan for Grand Canyon National Park (established as such in 1919), Lookout Studio "...seems of the rim itself." Low stone walls lead up to the building, protecting visitors from drop-offs, and the enclosed observation room is reached via a small stairway with log newel posts and railing. An exterior viewing deck was built below the main level. But views are what Lookout Studio is about, and large windows open the structure.

Phantom Ranch (1922)

In 1916, Colter began the design of Indian Gardens, the company's first project to be built within the canyon, along Bright Angel Trail. The project was shelved, but she worked tirelessly on other Santa Fe/Harvey projects. In

1922, she used the Indian Garden concept to design the lodge at Phantom Ranch and a group of four two-person cabins that created an oasis, deep within the canyon and next to Bright Angel Creek. These modest rock-and-frame buildings, in keeping with new national park building policy and Colter's own aesthetic, seemed hidden in their setting. Additional building, this time in board and batten, expanded the "ranch" in 1927-1928, when eight new guest cabins and a dining hall were constructed.

The Watchtower at Desert View (1932)

Visitors to Colter's other buildings felt as if they had stepped into another world: that of a hermit, a Hopi Indian, an explorer. At Watchtower, they stepped back in time. With the automobile now a popular form of transportation, Watchtower could be built far from the maddening crowds of the

Herman Schweizer on a research trip with Mary Colter poses at Round Tower in Cliff Palace, Mesa Verde National Park. Grand Canyon National Park Museum, No. 16968.

South Rim and Grand Canyon Village, and be enjoyed in relative solitude. Colter knew she wanted to re-create an ancient Indian tower, so she chartered a small plane to spot tower ruins, then rode in Harvey-provided cars to check them out. Her six months of research included extensive visits to Hovenweep National Monument and Mesa Verde National Park, where she found inspiration in the cliff dwellings, particularly Mesa Verde's Round Tower of Cliff Palace.

She sketched out the plan and built a clay model. A 70-foot wooden tower was constructed at the site, so Colter, now in her sixties, could climb to the platform to make sure the site and height were correct. While the tower's inspiration was ancient, the tapered cylinder was built over a steel-frame structure on a concrete foundation. Local rock created a richly textured surface.

The exterior may be stunning, but Colter saved the best for inside. By

Top Photo: The Desert View Watchtower.
Xanterra. *Above: Mary Colter looking out a door of Twin Tower on one of her research trips.*
Grand Canyon National Park Museum, No. 13315.

now, her knowledge of Native American art was extensive and she was ready to use it. The walls became canvases, and Hopi painter Fred Kabotie, under the direction of the "quite elderly Miss Colter," shared Hopi legends and the spirituality of his people for generations to enjoy. Joining Kabotie was Harvey artist Fred Geary, who replicated pictographs and petroglyphs from sites that Colter and Harvey Indian Department manager Schweizer had visited. Most stunning was the tower's panoramic

view of the canyon and surrounding plateau.

The tower was completed in 1932, but the official opening was delayed until May 13, 1933. Of all of Mary Colter's work at the Grand Canyon, Watchtower seems to be her lavish thank-you to the Native Americans who so inspired her. The Watchtower's official opening-day dedication was a Hopi blessing called *De-Ki-Veh*. According to Frank Waters, author of *Masked Gods*, two days prior, the Hopis held their own dedication ceremony, and Mary Colter was the only white person present.

Bright Angel Lodge (1935)

Since 1917, two years before the Grand Canyon became a national park, a working plan had been in place for the South Rim and Grand Canyon Village. That plan was fine-tuned in 1924 by the National Park Service and the Santa Fe Railway, with input from Mary Colter.

Part of the 1917 plan called for a

cottage community with a lodge and cabins to replace the old hotel, various unappealing cabins, and tent sites around El Tovar. Various cabins were moved or demolished; the original Buckey O'Neill Cabin, the oldest surviving structure on the rim, was preserved.

Colter drew up preliminary plans for a domed stone lodge on the rim, but they were rejected. Undaunted, she came back with a rustic, ranch-like, log-and-stone lodge to be surrounded by an eclectic assortment of cabins.

In December 1934, the architect returned to the Grand Canyon to oversee construction of the hotel that was taking shape. The low-slung lodge, where a huge overhanging porch covered the entry, offered a more neutral architectural palette than Colter's other trademark buildings. Guests were drawn to a massive fireplace of limestone interspersed with layers of other canyon stone and adorned with a painted Thunderbird. Flagstone floors and open truss ceilings, along with the rustic furnishings, reinforced a pioneer aura. The lodge opened on June 22, 1935, with an American West theme of barbecue and cowboys in addition to Hopi ceremonial dancers.

Interior of a Bright Angel Lodge Cabin as decorated by Mary Colter, 1936. Grand Canyon National Park Museum, No 16721b.

The lodge is impressive, but the quirky cabins with their collage of multicultural exteriors are absolutely charming. Log cabins are attached to stucco southwestern design. Bright colors highlight their doors, and guests wander down paths in search of their special overnight accommodation.

Men's (1936) and Women's (1937) Dormitories

In 1925, Colter had drawn up plans for a men's dormitory at the canyon and in 1936, the 52-room building was completed, with the women's quarters— later renamed Colter Hall—constructed the following year. They remain part of the Grand Canyon Village Historical District.

Mary Colter's work at the Grand Canyon evolved with the times, but held true—or defined—the tenets of National Park Service Park architecture.

Hopi Indian, Jimmy Kewanwytewa with Kachina doll. Courtesy of the Cline Library at Northern Arizona University, No. NAU.PH.98.38.5.

She embraced and promoted regionalism and Native American people and their art, respected with unwavering faith the landscape on which she worked, and all the while never let her eye roam from the commercial purposes of her buildings. As noted in the 1917 Grand Canyon Working Plan:

"As long as the Fred Harvey Company's work is passed upon to Miss Colter, its present architect, its appropriateness can be considered assured."

Hopi House Restoration (1995)

Over the years, after Mary Colter's defining presence was no longer a part of the Grand Canyon, Hopi House continued as the premier place to purchase and view Indian curios, art, and artifacts. Modernization, including installation of a sprinkler system, electrical connections in exposed conduits, and carpeting on the first floor, slightly altered the original building, but "…the

Above: A double lightning petroglyph from one of Mary Colter's research trips. Grand Canyon National Park Museum, No. 08318.

Below: Part of the Grand Canyon Village Historical District, the Women's Dormitory, completed in 1937, was renamed Colter Hall. Grand Canyon National Park Museum, No. 839.

historic flavor remains untouched," according to the 1976 National Register of Historic Places Inventory Nomination Form. The nomination included all of the historic furnishings and ceremonial objects.

Hopi House was designated a National Historic Landmark in 1987. In 1995, it underwent a $750,000 restoration and rehabilitation. According to Jim Woodward, of Woodward Architectural Group, who contracted to do the bulk of the work, most of the damage was weather related. Years of patch-and-repair on the roof had left a hodge-podge of decaying layers that was removed, giving the architect an opportunity to strengthen the floor and roof system. The Hopi House also needed to be retrofitted to meet earthquake standards.

"Putting on a proper roof went hand in hand with the structural work that we needed to do," explained Woodward. "Also, dismantling the stone parapets down to the roof joists was necessary since the sandstone parapets were pretty severely damaged. This gave us an opportunity to connect joists to stone walls, rebuild the parapets and put on the new roof and flashing."

Some of the sandstone at the base of the walls and along the parapets was replaced. With a little help from historians and archaeologists, quarries on land once owned by the Santa Fe Railway were found, and the stone was cut from "a quarry that was most likely used for the original stone, located near Winslow," said Woodward.

The original mortar was adobe mud. Spots had been repaired with Portland cement that added to the deterioration, so the new mortar was a combination of cement, sand, and lime. While most of the work was on the exterior, interior restoration included re-plastering the adobe mud, taking care not to disturb the Indian drawing. An additional stairway was installed to the second floor to meet new code. The sixty tiny windows were in fair shape, but their wood frames or sashes had to be tightened and restored.

Working in conjunction with the National Park Service and the Arizona State Historic Preservation Office to ensure authenticity, Grand Canyon National Park Lodges (Xanterra Parks and Resorts) conducted the renovation so as not to alter any of the original architectural or design elements. Several Hopi workmen participated in this restoration effort. The restoration/rehabilitation won the 1997 Governor's Awards for Historic Preservation in the commercial category.

"It [Hopi House] was a unique building for its time. I wouldn't think it was the first Pueblo revival building, but an idea Colter generated to deal with displaying and selling Indian art. Besides the accuracy of its design was literally creating a Pueblo living [environment]. From a tourist prospective, it was as real as you could get. Not just a building where Indian art was for sale, but an entire attempt to create a mini-culture."

Facing Page: Looking up through the parapets of the Watchtower to the ceiling artwork. Grand Canyon National Park Museum, No. Tdvi02.
Right: To this day, the Hopi House embodies the rich cultural and architectural environment of the Pueblo Indians. Xanterra, No. AH2003.

Indian Arts and Image

There is no doubt that the Santa Fe Railway and Fred Harvey Company romanticized Native Americans and their culture in their marketing and advertising campaigns. By the early part of the 20th century, the Santa Fe and other railways had changed the image of Indians, and that of the West's wilds as a whole, from a frightening aspect of American life to one of intrigue. Expositions and destination fairs recreated these worlds in miniature, giving fair visitors a manageable dose of these totally foreign landscapes and the Native Americans who inhabited them.

As for the art depicting the region, the confluence of the physical beauty of the Southwest, particularly the Grand Canyon, and the physical beauty of the native peoples and their art seemed to carry equal weight. The paintings of Anglo artists shared a rich and exotic glamour in their interpretation of what appeared to be a new utopia. That interpretation was widely used by William Simpson in promotional materials, including framed lithographs, magazine covers, playing cards, books and the famous Santa Fe Railway calendars that, beginning in 1907, brought a face of the Southwest into 300,000 homes, offices, and schools.

Renowned potter Nampeyo with two children. Her pieces were greatly sought by collectors. *Grand Canyon National Park Museum, No. 9826.*

The Indians' arts and crafts, rooted in their spiritual world, were exquisite, earthy, and natural, with ceremonial and religious overtones. Intricate pottery patterns fashioned from ancient shards, ceremonial masks and Kachinas (dolls that embody the spirits of the living and dead, and possess powers over nature) were integral parts of Indian spiritual and everyday life. Silver jewelry, baskets, rugs, and blankets often incorporated spiritual designs. Subjects and techniques of paintings, drawings, and pictographs evolved in style and content as the Indian cultures were altered by "Americanization."

Travel writers and advertising copy offered something else. With El Tovar and Hopi House completed, in 1905 William Simpson penned *El Tovar, By Fred Harvey: A New Hotel at Grand Canyon of Arizona.* The copy about Hopi House is unapologetically chauvinistic:

"A short distance east of el Tovar and a stone's throw from the sheer canyon wall is the Hopi House, an irregular stone structure, plastered with adobe...that looks like an Indian pueblo; and so it is, in miniature...These quaintly-garbed Indians on the housetop hail from Twewa, the home of Nampeyo, the most noted pottery-maker in all Hopiland. Perhaps you are so fortunate to see Nampeyo herself.

"Here are Hopi men, women, and children—some decorating and burning exquisite pottery, others spinning

The start of a beautifully patterned basket. Denver Public Library, Western History Collection, No. X30891.

Hopi Indians from neighboring Pueblos gather on the roof garden of the Hopi House. Grand Canyon National Park Museum, No. 9847.

yarn and weaving squaw dresses, scarfs and blankets. Go inside and you see how these gentle folk live. The rooms are little and floors and walls are as cleanly [sic] as a Dutch kitchen. The Hopis are making "piki" twining the raven black hair of the "manas" in big side whorls, smoking corn-cob pipes, building sacred altars, mending moccasins—doing a hundred un-American things…It is almost as good as the trip the province of Tusayan, minus the desert."

More to the point, George Wharton James wrote in his 1910 book, *The Grand Canyon of Arizona: How to See It*, that Hopi House offered:

"…an education in the customs, arts, history, mythology, religious ceremonials, and industries of not only one, but many tribes of Indians. It is not only a good business investment, but a place of benefit to which one should go prepared intelligently to study. Such as one will come away with a keen appre-

"Manas" pose in native costume with their hair in maiden side whorls. Denver Public Library, Western History Collection, NO. X30790.

The intricate silver work of Southwest Indian jewelry evokes spiritually and culturally inspired designs. Mary Colter was an avid collector of such pieces. Courtesy Linda McCray.

ciation of the incomparable ethnological advantages this building affords him, and he will not grudge any purchases, however, large, the attractiveness of the display has led him to indulge in."

The Indian arts collection of the Fred Harvey Company was not your usual curio shop fare. Under the direction of Harvey executive John Huckel, with Herman Schweizer in the field, the company acquired one of the most impor-

tant collections of Indian arts and artifacts in the country. Not only did the Harvey Company stock its own warehouse in Albuquerque, the museums in Indian House and Hopi House, and shops at their various venues, but also

it bought from and sold to institutions including the Berlin Museum, the Field Columbian Museum in Chicago, the Carnegie Museum in Pennsylvania, and wealthy clients such as newspaper tycoon William Randolph Hearst. Schweizer began collecting native arts at the end of the 19th century, but according to Byron Harvey III in *The Fred Harvey Company Collects Indian Art: Selected Remarks,* early ledger entries on acquisitions began in July 1903 with the purchase of fourteen Hopi Kachina dolls and eleven sacred masks (sacred mask purchases were curtailed). Those purchases were a minute indication of the volume of collectibles Schweizer

Indians worked these hand-looms demonstrating their craft. Today, quality rugs and weavings can still be purchased at the Hopi House. Xanterra, No. AH1965.

acquired from Indians, trading posts, other noted collectors, ethnologists, and archaeologists through the first half of the 20th century. Schweizer's collecting went beyond Indian materials, and included Spanish Colonial artifacts. While many museum-quality pieces were sold, it was company policy to keep in storage a wealth of prime items in a vault at the Alvarado hotel location. These were for posterity and investment, and served as models for reproductions sold at Harvey shops. Schweizer was also credited with commercializing Navajo silver by purchasing fine examples that were copied and sold. One of his enthusiastic collectors was Mary Colter.

Schweizer was interested in quality workmanship. Hopi potter Nampeyo was hired to demonstrate her craft at the opening of Hopi House. Schweizer found that she had not brought enough high-grade clay, whereupon he had clay gathered and shipped from her home

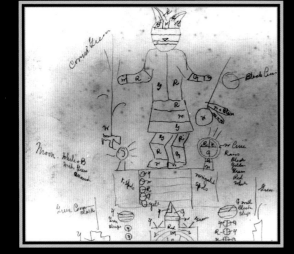

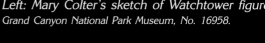

Left: Mary Colter's sketch of Watchtower figure.
Grand Canyon National Park Museum, No. 16958.

Below Left: A ceremonial altar with sand
painting. Denver Public Library, Western History
Collection, No. X30771.

Below: Fred Kabotie worked closely with Mary
Colter in painting much of the interior of the
Watchtower. Grand Canyon National Park Museum,
No. 8307.

Left: Indians were on hand to interpret the many figures and murals that adorned the walls of the Watchtower. *Grand Canyon National Park Museum, No. 8504.*

Below Left: Petroglyph of three deer photographed on one of Colter's research expeditions. *Grand Canyon National Park Museum, No. 08303.*

Above: Maize/meander petroglyph. *Grand Canyon National Park Museum, No. 08316.*

Einstein and wife pose at the Hopi House, Grand Canyon National Park Museum, No. 05118.

Herman Schweizer mingles with Hopi men preparing to perform for tourists. Grand Canyon National Park Museum, No. 16946.

to the Grand Canyon. Other Indian artisans, including potters Maria and Julian Martinez, Frank Katobie, and Elle and Tom of Ganado, were hired and worked for decades for the Harvey Company. So did the well-known medicine man Miguelito, who created sand paintings, according to scholar Kathleen L. Howard. Other Indian "consultants"

were hired to assist and educate Harvey buyers in the field.

Schweizer's interest in Indian art extended to the ceremonies, chants, and dances performed for guests.

Schweizer helped to arrange the dedication of the Harvey buildings, but his reach included the dedication of the Grand Canyon as a National Park. On April 30, 1920 (a year after Grand Canyon was designated a national park), a park dedication at El Tovar included scripting for Hopi participation planned by Schweizer. Schweizer was also on hand for photo opportunities, probably the most unusual being the visit by Professor Albert Einstein and his wife, who posed with Hopi Indians, a Santa Fe Railway agent, and Herman Schweizer.

Thomas Moran's painting, The Grand Canyon of the Colorado, was a widely distributed advertising image for the Santa Fe Railway. Grand Canyon National Park Museum, No. 13469.

The manager's passion for collecting was legendary, and it continued into the Depression. Schweizer died in 1943; in 1968 the Fred Harvey Company was sold to Amfac, Inc. (now Xanterra Parks and Resorts) and the collection was vested in "The Fred Harvey Fine Arts Collection." That collection was eventually given to The Heard Museum in Phoenix, Arizona, along with the company papers. Mary Colter's jewelry collection was bequeathed to Mesa Verde National Park in Colorado, where it is on exhibit.

Hopi House stands today as one of the signature structures that define Grand Canyon National Park architecture. Mary Colter's work merges like the confluence of two great rivers: on the one hand is its very commercial aspect, and on the other are the exquisite cultural, natural, and architectural influences she drew from.

Following Page: Sunset from Bright Angel Point, Grand Canyon. David M. Morris.

Mary Colter's canyon-inspired stonework at Hermit's Rest. Xanterra, No. AH2299.

Books

Albright, Horace and Robert Cahn. The Birth of the National Park Service: The Founding Years, 1913-33 (Salt Lake City, 1985).

Anderson, Michael. Living at the Edge (Grand Canyon, 1998).

Barnes, Christine. Great Lodges of the West (Bend, OR: W. W. West, 1997)

_____ Great Lodges of the National Parks (Bend, OR: W. W. West, 2002).

_____ El Tovar at Grand Canyon National Park (Bend, OR: W. W. West, 2001).

Berke, Arnold. Mary Colter: Architect of the Southwest (New York, 2002)

Bradley, Glen. The Story of the Santa Fe (Boston, 1930; reprint, 1995).

D'Emillo, Sandra and Suzan Campbell. Visions & Visionaries: The Art and Artists of the Santa Fe Railway (Salt Lake City, 1991).

Grattan, Virginia L. Mary Colter: Builder Upon the Red Earth (Flagstaff, 1980).

Henderson, James David. Meals by Fred Harvey A Phenomenon of the American West (Fort Worth, 1969)

Hughes, Donald, J. In the House of Stone and Light (Grand Canyon, 1991).

Howard, Kathleen and Diane Pardue. Inventing the Southwest, the Fred Harvey Company and Native American Art (Flagstaff, 1996).

James, Henry. Pages from Hopi History (Tucson, 1974).

Kaiser, Harvey H. Landmarks in the Landscape (San Francisco, 1997).

McClelland, Linda Flint. Building the National Parks (Boston & London, 1998).

Thomas, D.H. The Southwestern Indian Detours (Phoenix, 1978).

Waters, Fred. Masked Gods (Chicago, 1950). _____. Book of the Hopi (New York, 1963).

Weigle, Marta, and Barbara Babcock, eds. The Great Southwest: The Fred Harvey Company and the Santa Fe Railway (Phoenix, 1996).

Reports and Periodicals

Chappell, Gordon. "Railroad at the Rim: The Origin and Growth of the Grand Canyon Village." The Journal of Arizona History, Vol. 17, No. 1 (1976).

Grand Canyon National Park Museum Collection, Grand Canyon, AZ: El Tovar by Fred Harvey, A New Hotel at the Grand Canyon, 1905; Titan of the Chasms: The Grand Canyon of Arizona, 1904; Doing the Grand Canyon, 1909; The Grand Canyon of Arizona: How to See It, 1910; Correspondence of Atchison, Topeka & Santa Fe, 1902-1911; Santa Fe Railway promotional brochures, 1928-1932; History file, Fred Harvey Company, The Fred Harvey Collection: 1889-1963.

Grand Canyon Village Historic District, National Register of Historic Places Form, 1990.

Harrison, Laura Soulliere, "National Register of Historic Places Inventory Nomination Form, El Tovar and Indian Watchtower at Desert View, Lookout Studio, Hopi House, Hermit's Rest." (San Francisco: National Park Service, Southwest Regional Office, 1986).

The Santa Fe Magazine, May 1924 through February 1942, courtesy of Gordon Chappell, National Park Service, Western Regional Office, San Francisco.

Tweed, William, Laura E. Soulliere, Henry G. Law. National Park Service Rustic Architecture: 1916-1942 (San Francisco: National Park Service, Western Regional Office, February 1977).

Woodward Architectural Group, Phoenix. "Project Description: Use of Masonry in Design, Commercial Restoration/Rehabilitation of Hopi House at the Grand Canyon," 1997.